JAMAICA

Likkle, but Tallawah!

Diary of a Traveling Black Woman:
A Guide to International Travel

"Mini Travel Guide Series"
Volume III - Jamaica
2nd Edition

Jamaica:
Likkle, but Tallawah!

Shadeyka Warren

The Traveling Black Women Network
Grace Royal International, LLC
Atlanta, GA

Cover Model: Shadeyka Warren
Cover Design: Nadine C. Duncan
Interior Design: Nadine C. Duncan

ISBN: 979-8-9862680-0-2
ISBN: 979-8-9862680-1-9 (eBook)

2nd Edition, June 2022
Travel Guide Series, Volume III
Printed in the United States of America

Published in the United States by:
The Traveling Black Women Network
Grace Royal International, LLC
Atlanta, GA 30316

www.travelingblackwomen.com

For My Melanin Sisters All Around the Globe and My Ancestors Who Slaved on The Sugar Plantations of Jamaica

"Everyone has a special gift they can contribute to making this world a better place, and your gift may or may not be a solo trip away from discovery."
-Gloria Atanmo

CONTENTS

WHAT YOU NEED TO KNOW

Rockhouse Hotel
Negril, Jamaica

Photographer: Rita Bahiense

Jamaica Mon! The History.

Jamaica gained its independence from Great Britain in 1962. Like many newly independent nations, the country struggles financially. I am a huge advocate for being culturally aware when traveling, and as such, I think it is extremely important to understand the social and political climate of a country before visiting. So, let's be honest… Jamaica is a country that is mainly dependent on tourism dollars and remittance payments as its biggest source of income. Jobs are far and few between, and wages are low. I wholeheartedly encourage you to spend your tourist dollars and support the local communities! We will discuss more of how you can do so later in the guide. But first, a little background…

Jamaica is a small island nestled in the beautiful blue waters of the Caribbean Sea. The island sits perfectly between Haiti on its right and Cuba on its left. It is the fourth most populous country in the Caribbean, with a population of just under three million people. However, don't take the island's small size for granted! There is a common saying in Jamaica that goes, "We likkle, but we tallawah!" When translated, this means "We are a small nation, but we are strong, fearless, and not to be underestimated!" Jamaica truly lives up to this saying. The island is bursting with culture, flavor, fun, and a beautiful aura that makes it a repeat destination on my vacation calendar. Most of all, the country is dripping with melanin magic! Jamaica's population is approximately 92% Black, with the other 8% accounting for various ethnic groups including Mixed Race, Chinese, Indian, and White.

Jamaica was originally inhabited by the Arawaks--an indigenous tribe who named the island Xaymaca. The Arawaks led a peaceful existence until their population was largely destroyed by the arrival of Colombus in 1494. Jamaica remained under Spanish rule until the Spanish were attacked by the British in 1655. Jamaica's sugar industry, built on enslaved labor, created substantial wealth for Great Britain. Full emancipation was granted in 1838 after a series of slave revolts.

When To Go

Jamaica has incredibly beautiful weather, with temperatures ranging anywhere between 65° F to over 100° F. This makes it an ideal destination, regardless of the time of year!

December through April is considered high season in Jamaica, and this is the time of year when most tourists flock to the island to enjoy some fun in the sun. However, they'll also enjoy inflated prices. Resorts, hotels, and flights tend to be priced much higher during this time of year.

Tourism tends to slow down during mid-April to June. Nonetheless, the weather remains favorable, and prices are lower. If you prefer an un-crowded atmosphere, this may be the best time to visit.

June to November is considered low season in Jamaica, because it is hurricane season. While temperatures remain warm, the tropical island can experience very heavy episodes of rain during these months. Accommodations and flights tend to be the lowest during this time of year. If you don't mind a little bit of rain, the summer months are still a good time to visit – just monitor the weather forecasts and take the necessary precautions.

Preparing to Go

Visas

As of 2019, United States, UK, and Canadian citizens do not need a visa to travel to Jamaica. However, if you are a citizen of the Cayman Islands, Haiti, Nigeria, Benin, or Cameroon, you need to obtain a visa prior to arrival. Rules can always change, be sure to check the embassy website before your trip.

Vaccinations

The Center for Disease Control recommends the standard vaccinations. These are the vaccinations that many of us most likely already received as a child. However, please be sure to double check with your medical provider before traveling. At the time of publication, Jamaica did not require COVID vaccinations to visit. However, guidelines for COVID Vaccinations change regularly, be sure to check the embassy website for the most updated information on vaccinations in Jamaica before your trip.

Travel Insurance

Travel insurance is a personal choice, but highly recommended since the pandemic. Some credit cards will automatically cover the cost of a cancelled trip, but may not include hospital fees if you were to get hurt or ill or have strict guidelines. Some US health insurance plans also extend to international care. It's important to know what you have before leaving. If you find you need to purchase a separate plan, they are relatively inexpensive. Scan the QR code below to compare insurance plans.

MBJ/KIN

Jamaica has two major airports that service travel to and from the island. The first is **Sangster International Airport (MBJ),** located on the northwest coast in Montego Bay. This is the airport that most vacationers fly into, as it is closest to the popular tourist hubs and resorts. You would fly into this airport if you will be staying in Montego Bay, Ocho Rios, or Negril.

The second airport is **Norman Manley International Airport (KIN),** located on the southeast coast in Kingston. This airport is more frequented by locals and citizens visiting from abroad, as it is located closer to populated inner-city communities. However, you would be flying into this airport if you will be staying in Kingston or Port Antonio.

Packing

As I mentioned earlier, Jamaica maintains a hot tropical climate all year round. It is always summer in Jamaica! If you are like me and from a bitter cold city like New York, you will definitely appreciate the warm sun. Feel free to pack the same types of clothing that you would wear during summer months in your own hometown – light breathable fabrics, t-shirts, shorts, dresses, swimsuits, and sandals. If you plan on doing physical activities such as hiking, be sure to pack comfortable sneakers. You may also want to include accessories such as sunglasses and straw hats, if that's your style. Jamaica is a very liberal country, and you will not have to worry about adhering to any strict religious or social dress customs.

I also highly recommend bringing sunscreen and mosquito repellent (the mosquitoes are deadly, okay!) You may also want to bring travel sized medications in case you come down with any unfortunate illnesses. I never travel without over the counter pain meds, meds for an upset stomach, and meds for my allergies.

Packing List:

To Do List:

Hellshire Beach ~ Kingston, Jamaica
Models (left to right): Tramaine Blyden, Malika Stephens

WHAT TO EXPECT

Jamaican Culture

WAH GWAN?

The official language of Jamaica is English. The English spoken in Jamaica is strongly influenced by British English (because they were colonized by the British, remember?!). Nonetheless, you should have absolutely no problem communicating.

Widely spoken in Jamaica is a dialect of English known as 'Jamaican Patois' (pronounced "pat-wah"). If you have ever heard a Jamaican person speak, then you likely already know what I'm talking about! Jamaican Patois is an English based creole language, developed during the era of slavery, that is a distinctive fusion of English, Spanish, and West African languages. It is a unique dialect, and the cornerstone of Jamaican culture.

Jamaicans tend to talk very fast, which can make Patois difficult to understand if you are not used to hearing the dialect. If you listen and pay very close attention, you may definitely be able to decipher what they are saying.

Jamaican Patios Phrases

- "Wah Gwan?" - What's Up?
- "Walk Good!" - Bye
- "Soon Come!" - On the way
- "Irie" - Chill/Good
- "Big Up!" - Great Job
- "Respect" - Great Job
- "Nuh rump wid me" - Don't play with me
- "Small Up yourself" - Get out of the way
- "Seen" - I get it
- "Bredren" - Brother/Homie

Food!!!

Mmmm, my favorite part of the book! Jamaican food is Bangin' (with a capital B)! The blends of spices, flavors, and aromatic essences will have your mouth watering during your entire trip. I guarantee you.

Firstly, y'all know I have to encourage healthy eating; so, be sure to eat as many fresh juicy fruits as you can. Jamaica is a tropical island, with an abundance of natural, organic foods. This is your time to eat organically without paying fancy organic prices! Mangoes, guava, bananas, cherries – eat it all! You may even want to step outside of the box and try some tropical fruits like Otaheite apples, guineps, and june plums.

Now, on to the good (or bad) stuff! Jamaicans are known to heavily season and spice their foods. In almost every dish, you will find strong flavors of garlic, allspice, scotch bonnet pepper, and thyme. You will also find that Jamaican cuisine is usually very heavy, regardless of the time of day.

A typical breakfast may consist of ackee – Jamaica's national fruit – cooked with codfish, and served with fried or boiled dumplings (flour and water mixture), fried yellow plantains, boiled green bananas, and other root vegetables such as cassava and yams. Another favorite breakfast item is porridge cooked of cornmeal, oats, banana, or other grains. You may also find dishes such as stewed kidney, liver, or mackerel fish. Don't knock it until you try it!!!

Lunch and dinner dishes will consist of a variety of meals including jerk chicken, curried chicken or goat, stewed chicken or beef, stewed oxtails, fresh fried or roasted fish, and soups. The soups in Jamaica are not your typical chicken noodle; they are heavy and hearty soups made with beef or chicken, a variety of root vegetables, dumplings, corn, and lots of flavor.

You will find that meat dishes are typically paired with Jamaican rice and peas – traditionally made with coconut milk, thyme, allspice, and other seasonings. Other starches include bammy (a cassava-based flatbread) and festival (similar to fried dumplings, but made with cornmeal and sugar).

If you are looking for a quick snack, be sure to try an authentic Jamaican patty! There are plenty of chain restaurants such as 'Tastee', 'Juici Patties', and 'Mother's Patties', where you will be able to get the most delicious beef, chicken, or veggie patties that you've ever had! Other popular snack items are plantain chips, banana chips, coconut drops, and tamarind balls. If you will be visiting during the Easter season, be sure to try fresh baked bun and cheese. Bun is a traditional, sweet and savory pastry bread that is often eaten with locally-made cheese.

No, I did not forget my vegan [and vegetarian] sisters! The Rastafarian religion is heavily practiced in Jamaica, and "Rastas", as they are called, eat primarily vegan dishes known as "ital food". You should have no problem finding a plethora of options to fit your diet.

Drugs/Alcohol

The legal drinking age in Jamaica is 18 years old. Jamaica's popular alcoholic spirits include Appleton Rum, Wray and Nephew Overproof Rum and Rum Cream, Sangster's Rum Cream, and Campari Bitter. The most popular beer is Red Stripe, which comes in a variety of flavors including lager, sorrel, and lemon. Jamaicans also enjoy Dragon Stout and Magnum Tonic Wine, which are rumored to be aphrodisiacs (but I wouldn't know......).

Contrary to popular belief, **marijuana is illegal** in Jamaica. In 2015, the Jamaican government decriminalized the possession of up to two ounces of marijuana as only a petty offense, punishable by a small fine. You are likely to see many people smoking and selling marijuana (also known as herb, ganga, and bush). For many people, especially those who practice the Rastafarian religion, smoking marijuana is a part of daily life, and is seen as a religious rite.

The Jamaican government has made strong strides to discourage the use of the plant. However, marijuana still happens to be widely accepted by many people. While some tourists are eager to visit Jamaica to try the marijuana that they've heard others rave about, please be aware that it is illegal!

Being A Woman in Jamaica

Depending on your definition of harassment, you may or may not experience harassment in Jamaica. Let me just say this, Jamaican men are smooth talkers! They will flirt super hard, talk your ears off, and shower you with more compliments than you've probably ever received in your life. Not all of them, but many. Don't take it personally, it is just in their nature. For some this may be overwhelming and uncomfortable, while others may be flattered and entertained.

If you are in heavily populated tourist areas, be prepared to be haggled by locals trying to sell you things, from t-shirts to keychains to massages. They are just trying to make a living. Again, don't take it personally. If you are not interested in purchasing anything, a firm no should suffice.

In terms of safety, take the normal precautions that you would anywhere else in the world. Jamaica is a beautiful country; however, it is not 100 percent safe. Where there is poverty, there is crime, and Jamaica is no exception. If you are traveling with a group, stick together. Do not wander off into unknown areas of town alone. If you are traveling alone, someone you trust back home should know where you are at all time. Keep your belongings in sight, remain aware of your surroundings, and trust your gut instincts!

Money

Jamaica has their own currency – the Jamaican dollar. This is primarily used by locals. Most hotels and vendors in tourist areas will accept U.S., U.K., and Canadian currency, although U.S. is most popular. In fact, some tourist places will only accept payments in USD. In tourist areas, you will find that many things are priced in American dollars. However, when you begin to explore more local areas and establishments, items will be priced in Jamaican currency.

If you plan to stay on a resort and within the tourist hubs, there will be no reason to exchange your money. However, if you plan to venture outside of these areas, I highly suggest converting your money to Jamaican dollars. This way, you will get more bang for your buck due to the fact that the U.S. dollar is strong.

The rule of thumb for many travelers is that you never exchange money at the airport – issa scam! There are money exchange facilities called "cambios" all over Jamaica. If you are patient enough, visit a few of them to see where you can get the best exchange rate. Historically, the USD to JMD exchange rate has ranged between 1 USD = 110-130 JMD. A quick search before your trip will let you know what the current exchange rate is at your time of visit. You can also use ATMs that are compatible with your bank.

Credit cards are accepted at the airport, most hotels, and some fancier establishments. However, I would not suggest this method of payment. Cash is best. Additionally, consider keeping smaller bills ($1, $5, $10) on hand to tip your service providers throughout your trip. This goes a long way, and is a well appreciated gesture.

Staying Connected

Don't worry, you will not have to give up your phone or your beloved Social Media while you are away. Most hotels and Airbnbs provide free WiFi to help you stay connected. Some restaurants and establishments will also provide free WiFi; KFC is one of them (don't ask me how I know). You can make calls and send messages to anyone, anywhere using the 'WhatsApp' app on your smartphone. The person must also have the app downloaded to receive your communications. If you exchange numbers with any locals in Jamaica, it is highly likely that you will end up communicating via WhatsApp.

If WiFi is not enough for you, you can purchase a local SIM card at a phone store like 'Digicel' or 'Flow', which can be used if you have an unlocked smartphone. Along with the SIM, you can buy a prepaid plan (known as "credit") for $5-40 USD, depending on how much usage you need. The SIM card provides you with a local phone number, free incoming calls, text messaging, and outgoing usage charged to your prepaid limit. You can also just pay your cellphone company directly for a roaming plan. But why do that when there are more affordable options?!

Transportation/Navigation

I have one word to describe the driving in Jamaica: Crazy! Jamaicans are known to be some of the most reckless and dangerous drivers. The traffic laws are very different than abroad, as well as the street lights and signage rules. Before you decide to rent a car, please consider the following:

Firstly, Jamaicans drive on the right side of the road. If you do not or have never driven on the right side of the road, do not assume that it is easy! Infrastructure has improved over the years, and there are now major highways that connect various cities. However, in some areas, the roads can be very bad. Many roads are narrow, easily flooded, and filled with potholes and debris. There can often times be a lot of traffic obstacles in heavily populated areas – think stray dogs, other animals, people, food carts, and fruit stands.

If you still decide to rent a car, several major car rental companies operate on the island. Keep in mind, however, that as of publication, there are no major credit card companies that cover rental car insurance in Jamaica. You will have to shell out some extra cash for the added security. You will definitely not want to bypass purchasing insurance, due to the fact that many local drivers operate without car insurance. So, if an accident unfortunately occurs, you do not want to be left stuck with a hefty bill.

An alternative option is to hire a private driver. Ask your hotel's front desk or Airbnb host to recommend a professional and reliable driver to you. Many hotels and hosts have drivers on call just for this purpose. Depending on your location, the size of your group, and itinerary, private driver rates can range anywhere from $30 to over $100 a day. This may be a much safer option for tourists, as private drivers are experienced, and know the roads and areas well.

Taxis

Rideshare companies, like Uber, are not yet widespread in Jamaica. However, taxis are readily available at the airport and all throughout the country. Many taxi drivers will try to inflate prices for tourists, so agree on a decent price before you hop in the car! Again, ask your hotel's front desk or Airbnb host to recommend reliable and reasonably priced taxi services. The Jamaica Union of Travelers Association (JUTA) is a network of officially registered tourism vehicles that provide taxi services primarily to tourists.

Some hotels will provide free shuttle service to and from the airport, and to popular destinations in the area. I have also had Airbnb hosts offer airport pickup and drop off for a small fee. Some will even do it for free! Check up on those details prior to travel.

Public Transportation

There are public bus routes that run throughout every city in Jamaica. The local transportation system can be difficult to navigate, as many bus stops are at unofficial locations with no signage, and you absolutely do not want to get lost in Jamaica. Also, most buses are not modern or comfortable, and do not have bells to indicate when you want to get off. Instead, you may find yourself yelling "Next Stop!" to the driver. If you are not used to this, it can be uncomfortable. Unless you will be moving to Jamaica or staying there long term, I do not suggest local public transportation. Although, if you are feeling adventurous, you may want to give it a try.

Knutsford Express

The Knutsford Express is a coach bus service that allows you to travel between cities around Jamaica for as little as $15 to $40 USD. The service is very reliable, with comfortable seats, air conditioning, WiFi, and electrical outlets. The drivers can sometimes be pretty entertaining as well! There are bus stations in every major city on the island, and at the airports.

Notes

Notes

Map of Jamaica
Illustrator: Kamrie McKay

WHERE TO GO

&

WHAT TO DO

Now that you're all hyped up and ready for your trip, we are on to the fun stuff… deciding which part of the country to go! Jamaica is such a dynamic destination that it would be almost impossible to cover every single city, attraction, and activity in this guide. Therefore, I will be focusing on the top five cities for visitors – Montego Bay, Ocho Rios, Port Antonio, Negril, and Kingston – in that order!

Where to Stay

Do you remember earlier in the guide when I discussed supporting the local people and communities? Well, using Airbnb is one of the best ways you can do so! This is a great way to support and connect with local people. I personally only stay in Airbnb's when I visit Jamaica. There are some very beautiful listings on the website that you can book for as little as $30 a night. Many homes come with great amenities, personalized service, and very friendly hosts. Some people are concerned with the safety of staying in a short term rental. If you are one of those people, my advice to you is to read the reviews! Read the entire listing description so that you can have an idea of what to expect, and read every review if you can. Also, search for "Superhosts," which are hosts that have been verified by Airbnb for having consistent, exceptional service.

Now, I am not knocking all-inclusive resorts. I think that they are a great option as well. You will not have to worry about anything – food, drinks, entertainment, and activities are all included in the price of your stay. Resorts are a good option for people who are worried about safety, since many have security on staff 24/7. I mainly suggest resorts for families, as there are many activities for kids to keep busy, and some even have babysitting services for parents who need a little alone time. Couples can also enjoy massages on the beach and spa services together.

If you prefer a catered all-inclusive experience, then a resort may be best for you. There are many options to choose from! However, I also can not personally recommend any particular resorts, since I have not stayed on any of them.

Before your trip, I encourage you to join the 'Traveling Black Women' Facebook group (if you have not already done so), and ask the ladies in the group what their top picks are! You are sure to get great responses and reviews. Additionally, I highly recommend www.tripadvisor. com for honest hotel reviews and traveler photos.

Local & Tourist Attractions

I will discuss some of the best places to visit, and most fun things to do. For some cities, I will also list a few of the many excursions offered by "Chukka Caribbean Adventures." Chukka is one of the leading tour operators in the Caribbean, with a strong presence in Jamaica, Turks and Caicos, Belize, Saint Lucia, and Antigua. The company has been around since the 1980's, and is well known for their professionalism, experienced tour guides, and entertaining excursions.

Where to Eat

Almost everywhere in Jamaica has delicious food. I can't name them all, or else this book would never end. However, I will give you my top three restaurant picks in each city! Please keep in mind that we are talking about Jamaica, meaning that everything (including food service) is much slower than abroad as everything is cooked to order. The food will be delicious, but don't expect to receive it in five minutes.

Nightlife

The turn up in Jamaica is definitely real, so believe the hype! Most all-inclusive resorts have nightly entertainment. However, if you are looking to get off of the resort (or if you aren't staying on one), I have you covered with my top picks in each city!

MONTEGO BAY
(AKA "MOBAY")

Doctor's Cave Beach
Montego Bay, Jamaica

Models (left to right):

Kennedy Harris, Cliniece Goodluck, Autasia Ramos, Brea Simons

LOCAL & TOURIST ATTRACTIONS

Doctor's Cave Beach

The most popular beach in Montego Bay, boasting beautiful white sand and crystal blue waters. Enjoy access to lifeguards, great food and drinks, and water activities (snorkeling, kayaking, jet ski, parasailing, etc). This is the perfect place for a beach day! Please note that there is a small entry fee.

Rose Hall Great House

A Georgian style mansion turned museum, Rose Hall is known for its impressive architecture and haunted history. Rose Hall was built in the 1700's, and sits on a former slave plantation with beautiful views of the city. The home is said to be haunted by the "White Witch of Rose Hall," and that's all I can tell you… You will have to visit to hear the full tale! It's quite interesting.

Martha Brae River Rafting

Approximately 20 miles from Montego Bay is the Martha Brae River, which is situated in between a beautiful plot of virgin green land. The river stretches for three miles, and the wooden rafts are operated by licensed and experienced raft captains. This is the perfect activity to enjoy a relaxing stroll down the river, take in the beautiful scenery, learn about the history of Martha Brae, and even enjoy a swim in the fresh cool water.

Croydon In The Mountains

Croydon is a pineapple and citrus plantation, nestled in the Catadupa Mountains, about 20 miles outside of Montego Bay. The area offers panoramic views of the surrounding countryside, and a variety of tropical organic fruits for visitors to enjoy. Tours are offered several times a day to teach visitors about the rich history of the plantation.

Chukka Tours
(See full listings at chukka.com)

- Ziplining
- ATV Quad Safari
- Dune Buggy Safari
- Horse Ride and Swim
- Snorkeling
- River Tubing
- Catamaran Party Cruise
- Catamaran Sail to Ocho Rios or Negril

WHERE TO EAT

Marguerite's

Marguerite's is a fine dining restaurant by the sea, known for their deliciously fresh and locally sourced seafood. Staple dishes on their menu include a variety of fishes, lobster, calamari, and scallops. The restaurant also has a great wine list! I will warn you that the menu is not cheap; however, it is a wonderful setting for a special night out.

Scotchies/Pork Pit (Tie)

You definitely cannot leave Jamaica without eating jerk chicken (sorry vegans)! Scotchies and Pork Pit are two restaurants, serving up the most delicious and decadent jerk chicken and jerk pork. The meat is cooked on a traditional grill made of pimento tree wood, giving it that nice smoky flavor. Ask your server for sides of festival and roasted yam, with a little drizzle of jerk sauce over your meat – yum!

Usain Bolt's Tracks and Records

Usain Bolt is not only the world's fastest man. He is also a restaurateur! His restaurant, which has multiple locations, is an upscale sports bar with a great atmosphere. The menu is catered more towards the American folks. However, the food is still delicious, and it's a great place to wind down and grab some drinks after a long day of exploring.

NIGHTLIFE

The Hip Strip

The Hip Strip is essentially the city center of Montego Bay. It is where most of the restaurants, bars, and nightlife is located. Some notable spots are Margaritaville, Pier One, Blue Beat Ultra Lounge, and Taboo Nightclub. You can also just take a walk down the Hip Strip, and go into whichever establishment looks the most fun! Many bars and clubs have themed nights such as Ladies Night or Karaoke Night.

You will likely see flyers and signs posted all over town, promoting parties that are taking place during that week; so be on the lookout out for those! There are some events that take place every week, such as Thursday night beach parties, and the like. Also, make friends with the locals, as they will be able to tell you what events are going on during your stay. As always, be safe and don't go anywhere or do anything that seems sketchy. Trust your gut, even when being spontaneous!

Reggae Sumfest

Sumfest is an annual music festival, that usually takes place in July. It is a week long affair of various parties and events that are hosted all throughout Montego Bay. The week ends with two massive concerts, with performances by popular reggae and dancehall artists. The festival has been taking place since 1993, and has featured artists such as Spice, Vybz Kartel, Beenie Man, and Sean Paul. International artists such as Rihanna, Nicki Minaj, and Kanye West have also hit the stage in the past!

OCHO RIOS
(AKA "OCHI")

Dunn's River Falls
Ocho Rios, Jamaica

Model: Tracia Walker

LOCAL & TOURIST ATTRACTIONS

Dunn's River Falls

Dunn's River is one of Jamaica's national treasures, and is a must do while you are there! Start at the bottom, on a private beach, and climb your way to the top of the falls. There are several natural pools/lagoons along the route where you can stop to take a dip in the cool spring water. I would suggest bringing water shoes, as the rocks can be very slippery and hard on the feet.

Turtle River Falls

If you are looking for a more lowkey scene, Turtle River Falls is a great alternative to Dunn's River. The concept of climbing the falls is the same, but the attraction is much less crowded. The grounds are home to over 80 species of beautiful birds, which you have the option to feed and interact with. The landscape is vast and gorgeous, with colorful plants, flowers, and other lovely animals all about.

Dolphin Cove

Disclaimer: This is not an attraction that I am personally a fan of, since I do not believe in holding animals in captivity for human entertainment. However, I still included it here because who am I to tell someone what they can and cannot enjoy?! Dolphin Cove is a huge attraction for families and children. You can participate in activities such as swimming and interacting with the dolphins. There are also other animals that you can interact with such as stingrays, sharks, and exotic birds. Additionally, there is a private beach that you can enjoy, along with other amenities.

Mystic Mountain

Mystic Mountain is an adventure park located within a tropical rainforest. The park's signature attraction is the Bobsled Ride, which starts with a 700ft high chairlift ride with great views of the city, and ends with an exhilarating bobsled roller coaster ride through the forest. The ride is inspired by Jamaica's bobsled team, who competed in several Olympic games. The park also offers ziplining, and guided tours of Dunn's River Falls.

Blue Hole

Blue Hole is a natural mineral spring and waterfall. You can swim in the fresh water, explore the different water holes, jump off of the cliffs, and take in the beautifully lush scenery. It is a hidden gem off the beaten path, and not as busy with people as Dunn's River. You may want to hire a driver to get here, since the roads leading to the grounds are not great.

Green Grotto Caves

About an hour outside of Ochi, this beautiful naturally formed cave is home to several species of animals and other organisms. There is a lot of history behind it, and the natural formations in the cave will have you in awe. The tour guides are really fun, and will have you laughing the entire time!

Chukka Tours
(See full listings at chukka.com)

- Ziplining
- Blue Hole and Cliff Jumping
- River Tubing
- Catamaran Sail to Dunn's River
- Bob Marley Cultural Experience Tour

WHERE TO EAT

Miss T's Kitchen

This colorful and rustic style restaurant is a great place to enjoy some authentic Jamaican food! The menu includes traditional meals like curry goat with rice and peas.

Dave's Lobster Shack

Omg! Amazing. I have never had seafood as fresh as this. Dave's gets their seafood fresh every morning, and prepares anything you want, anyway that you want it. My favorites are fried escovitch fish (served with a spicy pickle made of onions, peppers, and carrots) and the BBQ grilled lobster. However, you can get whatever you like. Most meals are served with festival, bammy, and plantains. Warning: You will not receive five-star dining and the food will take long, but it's worth the wait (don't say I didn't warn you).

Ocean's 11

A beautiful water front restaurant, with great views and an upbeat atmosphere. The menu includes traditional Jamaican dishes that are cooked to order. There is also an extensive menu of interesting cocktail concoctions, with names like "1-900-F*ck Me Up." The restaurant truly comes alive on Tuesday nights for Kara-oke. People from near and far will hit the stage to show off those vocals, and the hosts of the show are hilarious!

NIGHTLIFE

Some notable nightlife options:

- Oceans 11 – Karaoke Night
- Amnesia Night Club – Ladies Night
- Margaritaville – Pool Party
- Mongoose – Live Music
- Priory Beach Parties
- Shades Night Club --This is an adult club! Go with an open mind and you will have a blast!

At almost all of these venues, you will hear a mix of Dancehall, Reggae, Hip Hop, and R&B music. You may also hear some Top 40 songs mixed in. Similar to Mobay, Ochi will have posters all over town promoting different events that are taking place.

PORT ANTONIO
(AKA "PORTIE")

Frenchman's Cove Resort
Port Antonio, Jamaica

Model: Britishawna Petgrave

LOCAL & TOURIST ATTRACTIONS

Frenchman's Cove

Port Antonio is arguably the most beautiful part of Jamaica, and the sights to see do not disappoint. Frenchman's Cove is a beautiful turquoise green lagoon and stunning beach, all in one. The lagoon and sea eventually meet, which allows you to swim in both cold and warm water! The waters are decorated with swings and coves in the sea, making it a relaxing but fun experience for all. There is also a good restaurant on the beach where you can enjoy food and drinks.

Rio Grande River Rafting

Montego Bay is not the only place where you can experience picturesque bamboo river rafting. You can enjoy a calming ride down the Rio Grande River, as the expert raft captains entertain you with stories and tales of Jamaica and its history. The captains may even let you take over, and teach you how to drive the raft!

Blue Lagoon

This amazingly beautiful lagoon is fed by several underwater springs, and is a perfect place to spend an entire day. You can raft or you can hire one of the many locals to sail you around the bay. The water is a mix of warm and cold, and fresh and salt – it is a very weird combination that can only be experienced. Fun fact: There is a pond on the property that is said to have magical healing powers that will keep you from ageing if you swim in it.

Winnifred Beach

This is one of the most popular beaches in Port Antonio. It is a great place to relax, take in the sun, and eat some delicious jerk chicken from the local vendors. You may also want to do some snorkeling, since Port Antonio is home to some of Jamaica's most diverse coral reefs. On the beach, there are also several souvenir shops where you can purchase trinkets to take with you back home.

Reach Falls

Jamaica has dozens of amazing waterfalls, and this is one that you definitely want to experience! Reach Falls is a great excursion for adventure seekers. There are several holes within the falls that have been naturally carved out by the water. Brave visitors can jump into the holes, which takes them to secret underwater caves leading back to the main lagoon. If you aren't so brave, you can still have a fun waterfall experience by climbing the rocks, and enjoying the natural pools in between.

WHERE TO EAT

Wilkes Cuisine Seafood

Port Antonio has great seafood options, due to its proximity to the sea. Wilkes is a great place to enjoy a delicious meal, while overlooking the ocean. Don't be fooled by the outside – once you walk in, it is a cute and elegant restaurant where the food will not disappoint. The restaurant is well known for their curry seafood.

Soldier Camp

This restaurant is popular among locals and tourists alike. The menu consists of traditional authentic Jamaican food. If you want to try something different, go for the steamed snapper fish served with okra and Jamaican water crackers. Delish!

Cliff Hangar

Cliff Hangar is a beautiful restaurant located 100 feet above sea level, surrounded by beautiful lush plants and overlooking the Caribbean Sea. The menu is diverse, including Caribbean, American, vegan, and vegetarian dishes to suit any appetite. There is a full service bar serving up a variety of great drinks. You can grab a drink from the bar, and enjoy the beautiful atmosphere.

NIGHTLIFE

Port Antonio has a very relaxed and laid back vibe. The essence of the nightlife is also laid back, with most entertainment options being live music or chilling with drinks at a local bar. There are some lively nightclubs where you can dance to reggae and dancehall on a Friday or Saturday night. These include Roof Club, La Best Nightclub, and Cristal Nightclub.

NEGRIL

Seven Mile Beach
Negril, Jamaica

Model: Samantha Everette

LOCAL & TOURIST ATTRACTIONS

Seven Mile Beach

Negril is known for its incredible beaches – there are truly no others on the island like them. The sand is silky white, the waters are a bright iridescent blue, and the skies are almost always clear. The beach stretches for miles, and is filled with tons of activities and water sports for you to enjoy your day. The beach is very family friendly, and you will find a variety of dining and entertainment options. There are several all-inclusive resorts located along the beach as well.

Rick's Cafe

The famous Rick's Cafe! This is one of Jamaica's hot spots. Rick's is a restaurant and bar, located atop one of Negril's beautiful cliffs. However, most patrons don't actually go there for the food. They go for the thrilling cliff diving! There are several cliffs of different heights, and you will often find locals there who put on a show by diving off some of the highest cliffs.

Rick's also boasts some of the most beautiful sunsets on the island. At sunset, you will find all of the guests gathering near the balconies to enjoy the amazing uninterrupted view.

YS Falls

Some visitors call it the Dunn's River of Negril. YS Falls is a series of seven refreshing waterfalls, that cascade into several natural swimming pools. The waterfalls are surrounded by picturesque gardens, flowers, and trees. It is a great, family friendly activity.

Mayfield Falls

Mayfield is a great alternative to YS if you want to enjoy Jamaica's waterfalls. There are two waterfalls, with 21 natural pools, and 52 different species of exotic plants, birds, butterflies, and other wildlife. The grounds are kept immaculate, and is a good place for some Instagram worthy photos.

Appleton Rum Factory

If you like rum, then you will love this tour! A tour of the estate will teach you about the history of the Appleton brand, and the production process for creating the rum. During the tour, you will get to taste molasses and natural cane sugar. The tour ends with a tasting of over 10 different types of rums! The estate is located approximately 60 miles outside of Negril.

Floyd's Pelican Bar

Some people call it the coolest bar in the world. Why, you ask? Floyd's Pelican is a rustic floating bar in the middle of the Caribbean Sea! In order to get there, you have to take a 20-minute boat ride from the shore. Once there, you can enjoy – drink, swim, drink, eat, snorkel, and drink some more! It's okay if you aren't a great swimmer, because the water is very shallow there. The bar is decorated with memorabilia from visitors, such as flags, t-shirts, stamps, and even carved initials. Bring your own unique souvenir to add to the decorations!

Kool Runnings Adventure Park

Head to Kool Runnings to spend a fun family day! The park has a variety of activities to enjoy, including several water slides, tubing, water rides, go-kart racing, and paintball.

Chukka Tours
(See full listings at chukka.com)

- Ziplining
- Horse Ride and Swim
- Snorkeling
- Catamaran Party Cruise
- Tour of YS Falls

WHERE TO EAT

Rockhouse Restaurant

This restaurant, located at the Rockhouse Hotel, offers beautiful panoramic views of the perfectly blue sea and lush vegetation of Negril. The setting is rustic, yet elegant; and the menu includes a variety of Caribbean inspired dishes. You can have anything from an organic green smoothie to surf and turf cooked with fresh seafood. If you arrive early enough for dinner, you can experience one of Negril's most spectacular sunsets.

Sweet Spice Restaurant

This cute island-style restaurant offers some of the best traditional Jamaican cuisine. Menu options include dishes such as curry goat, stew chicken, and rice and peas. You can also choose from a variety of freshly blended juices such as fruit punch or sour sop juice (my fave!).

Fireman's Lobster Pit

Fireman's is a beachside spot known for their fresh lobster and crab. Customers have the opportunity to pick which lobster/crab they want from the live fresh catches of the day. The food is then cooked to your liking, and served with traditional items such as festival and plantains. The most popular dish is grilled lobster seasoned with garlic butter sauce.

NIGHTLIFE

Negril tends to have a very relaxed vibe most of the time, and nightlife is the most vibrant on the weekends. However, you can sometimes find events going on during the week. Some notable nightlife options are Margaritaville, The Jungle Nightclub, Alfred's Ocean Palace, Rick's Cafe, Bourbon Beach Bar, and Scrub-A-Dub Nightclub.

Dream Weekend

"Dream Weekend" is one of Jamaica's signature events. It is a week-long affair of various events and parties, and brings a high and vibrant energy to the otherwise laid-back vibe of Negril. The event takes place annually in August. Visit www.jamaicadreamweekend.com for more details.

KINGSTON

Carnival
(Xaymaca International Band)
Kingston, Jamaica

Model: Cinelli Mangal

LOCAL & TOURIST ATTRACTIONS

The Bob Marley Museum

If you know anything about the legendary Bob Marley, then you will absolutely love this museum! It is a tour of Bob's home, which is filled with incredible mementos that commemorate his career, and keeps his legacy alive. Guests will be guided throughout the entire property, including the inside and beautiful outside grounds of the home. The tour guides are very friendly and knowledgeable, and make the tour fun with stories, jokes, singing, and dancing! The tour ends with a 30-minute movie about Bob's life. I recommend this to anyone visiting Kingston.

Trench Town Culture Yard

Bob Marley is originally from an inner-city community called Trench Town, and the Culture Yard is the home where many of his famous hits were first created. This tour takes you through the different rooms in the home, which maintains some of the original furniture and artifacts from Bob's childhood. You will be able to learn about what life was like for people who lived in the yard during Bob's time, as well as what the community is like today. The yard is decorated with great artwork commemorating the life of Bob Marley and other great entertainers. If you are interested in learning about local life in Jamaica, this is a good tour to do.

Emancipation Park

Emancipation Park is famous for its statue of a naked male and female slave, which drew a lot of attention when the park fist opened. The park has beautiful scenery, and is a great place to take a stroll, jog, do yoga, have a cute picnic, or just relax. There are also sometimes different events being hosted at the park.

National Gallery of Jamaica

If you appreciate art, then you will definitely enjoy this display of incredible artwork! The National Gallery of Jamaica is the largest public art museum in the Caribbean, with a comprehensive collection of early, modern, and contemporary artwork from various Caribbean (mainly Jamaican) artists. The museum offers a wide variety of services including guided tours, speaking engagements, panel discussions, and children's programs. Some artwork and books are available for purchase as well.

The Blue Mountains

The mountains are by far my favorite location in Jamaica! Located about 45 minutes north of Kingston, The Blue Mountains' immense beauty will have you in awe. There are several guest homes available in the mountains, which you can find via Google or Air Bnb. There is only one notable hotel which is 'Strawberry Hill Hotel', however, it is a luxury property and the price can be upwards of $400 a night. There are plenty of activities and sites to enjoy up in the mountains including some national parks, hiking, nature walks, camping, and waterfalls; or you can just relax and enjoy the beautiful scenery around you! While you're there, be sure to try the amazing Blue Mountain coffee! The nearby John Crow Mountains offers similar activities.

Devon House

Devon House is a former slave plantation, turned cultural center. If you are interested in the history, you can take a tour of the big house, which is decorated with original 1800's British style furniture. However, most people really come to Devon House for the ice-cream! On the property, there are many shops, restaurants, and cafes. The Devon House "I Scream" parlor is by far the most popular! Some patrons have even dubbed it as the best ice cream in the world.

Carnival

Saving the best for last! This massive event only happens once a year! If you plan to be in attendance, hit the gym and get your stamina up, because you will be partying nonstop for several days straight! Carnival is a tradition that is celebrated in many Caribbean countries, and is a festive and colorful expression of Caribbean pride. The event includes weeks of various parties, which are hosted throughout the island. The celebration concludes with a huge street carnival, where men and women [of all shapes, colors, and sizes] dress up in festive attire and dance all day and night to the sweet lyrics of reggae, dancehall, and soca music. You can also join a formal "band", which is a company that provides carnival packages including a beautiful costume, food, drinks, entry to various events, and more.

WHERE TO EAT

Hellshire Beach

Hellshire is a local hotspot, where rustic-style restaurant stalls line the "beach" selling fresh seafood and authentic Jamaican fare. The reason I put "beach" in quotation marks is because Hellshire is less of a beach than it is a local hangout. The beach has been experiencing many years of unfortunate erosion, and there is little space to relax and play in the sand. Instead, people really go there for the delicious food. You will not see many tourists at Hellshire, as it is more popular amongst the locals. However, you may visit the nearby 'Fort Clarence Beach', where there is more beach, sand, and tourists. As such, there is a small entry fee (and way less food options).

Strawberry Hill Restaurant

The Strawberry Hill Hotel in the Blue Mountains has a beautiful restaurant, serving up a variety of multicultural dishes with a Jamaican twist. The best part about the restaurant is that you don't have to be a guest at the hotel to dine. This restaurant has the perfect setting and scenery to enjoy a classy brunch, while overlooking the stunning mountain views from the wraparound veranda.

KFC

Yes, you read that correctly. I would honestly be doing a disservice to you if I did not suggest one of the most prized restaurants in Jamaica. At any given time, in any area of Jamaica, you will find long lines of people (both inside and in the drive-through) of KFC. I don't know if it is the seasonings, the type of chickens, or the brand of oil that is used, but there is a reason why you can Google "Jamaica KFC" and find online threads titled "Why Does Jamaica Have the Best KFC in the World?" Some Jamaicans even joke that KFC is the country's national dish. (You can visit KFC anywhere on the island, but I decided to include it in this section because of its heavy popularity among Kingston locals.)

Sky Dweller Ultra Lounge (Bonus)

I will be honest and say that the food here is not my favorite. This is an upscale restaurant catered to tourists. Hence, the seasonings used and style of cooking is not authentically Jamaican. However, this restaurant/lounge has an extensive cocktail menu, with some delicious concoctions. Go here for the drinks and upbeat atmosphere!

NIGHTLIFE

Kingston is a bit different than the other cities in Jamaica, because it is the least touristy of them all. Hence, the nightlife is less dedicated to tourists, and more dedicated to the local crowd. In Kingston, most people decide where they are going to party for the night based on word of mouth, social media event promotions, and flyers posted around town. Most locals party locally – meaning that there are usually parties and dancehalls taking place within the inner communities that everyone knows about. For safety reasons, I would not suggest going to these unless you personally know or meet someone whom you trust!! However, if you ever have the opportunity to attend a local party, you will have the time of your life! This is where you will see colorful outfits and wigs, flying tables and chairs, women on their head tops, and all the crazy stereotypical Jamaican dancing that you've heard of. You can experience these parties anywhere in Jamaica; but Kingston is where most of them are concentrated.

There are several nightclubs that draw a more diverse crowd. However, if you aren't sure where and what is poppin' during your stay, you may end up partying all by your lonesome in an empty venue. My suggestion for Kingston is to ask the locals! They will definitely point you in the right direction, in terms of what is fun and safe for visitors. Nonetheless, some notable nightlife venues in Kingston are: Triple Century Sports Bar, Bacchanal Mas Camp, Club Escape, Club Riddim, Taboo Nightclub, and Pulse Nightclub.

ENJOY!

Note from the Author

I hope that this guide was able to provide all of the information that you need to begin planning your Jamaican getaway! If you visited Jamaica using the tips from this guide, I am interested to know how your trip went. Please feel free to send me an email at:

dizzydiscoveries@gmail.com.

Tell me all about your trip, and send pictures if you'd like! Additionally, you may send an email if you are interested in providing general feedback on the usefulness of this guide. You can also connect with me on Instagram (@dizzydiscoveries). I hope to hear from you soon!

About the Author
@dizzydiscoveries

hadeyka Warren (aka 'Dizzy') is a passionate travel blogger and writer. She was born and raised in Brooklyn, NY to Caribbean parents who introduced her to travel at the tender age of three. Her adventurous spirit and explorative nature has led her to countries such as Peru, Germany, Panama, and even Poland! However, her Caribbean roots has always brought her back to the West Indies, as a natural source of relaxation and the comforting feeling of "being at home." Shadeyka has spent several months at a time exploring the beautiful country of Jamaica, where she not only reconnected with extended family, but where she also learned the rich history of her ancestors who were once enslaved on the island.

Shadeyka currently curates photography and written content for her personal blog. As a Financial Advisor by trade, her blog not only covers travel, but financial literacy as well. Shadeyka is also a content contributor and writer for other blogs and websites that align with her goal and mission of uplifting women in the travel space. She hopes to continue creating enjoyable content, while encouraging people of color to get out and discover the world!

www.travelingblackwomen.com